D0573861

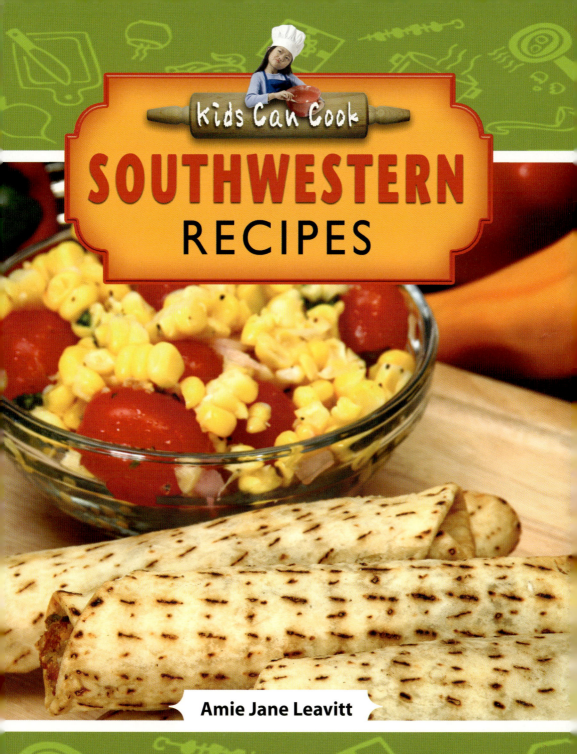

kids Can Cook

SOUTHWESTERN
RECIPES

Amie Jane Leavitt

Mitchell Lane
PUBLISHERS

kids Can Cook

Mid-Atlantic • Midwestern
New England • Pacific Northwest
Southwestern • Western
Recipes

Copyright © 2012 by Mitchell Lane Publishers

PUBLISHER'S NOTE: The facts on which this book is based have been thoroughly researched. Documentation of such research can be found on page 61. While every possible effort has been made to ensure accuracy, the publisher will not assume liability for damages caused by inaccuracies in the data, and makes no warranty on the accuracy of the information contained herein.

AUTHOR'S NOTE: Special thanks to my nephews and nieces (Isaac, Adda, Colby, Cameron, and Ava) for helping me make these recipes and for allowing me to take their photographs on so many occasions.

**Library of Congress
Cataloging-in-Publication Data applied for**

ISBN: 9781612280691

eBook ISBN: 9781612281636

Printing   1   2   3   4   5   6   7   8   9

PLB

THE MENU

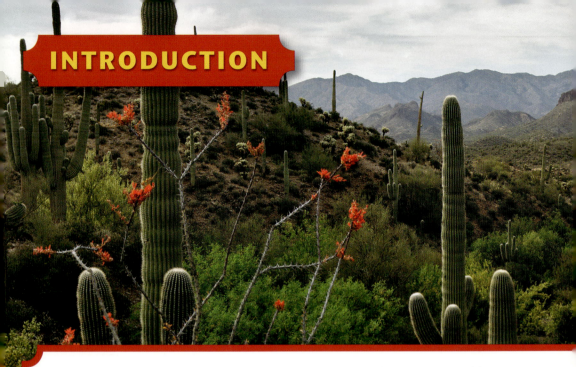

INTRODUCTION

Imagine a sandy desert landscape dotted with flowering prickly green cactuses, hopping jackrabbits, soaring hawks, red sandstone arches, and prehistoric cliff dwellings. By day the turquoise sky and golden rays of sunlight glorify this majestic landscape, and by night the lack of light pollution in the remotest parts of the desert allows the canopy of stars to sparkle like a brilliant sea of diamonds.

This is the American Southwest—the area of the United States that was once controlled by Spain and Mexico. It covers the modern states of Texas, New Mexico, Arizona, and California, and parts of Nevada, Utah, and Colorado. This book focuses on traditional foods from Texas through Southern California. Another book in this series, *Western Recipes,* takes a closer look at the cuisine from the rest of California, Nevada, Utah, and Colorado.

Anasazi, Hopi, Navajo, and other groups of Native Americans originally inhabited the Southwest. When the Spaniards arrived in the 1500s, they began setting up Catholic missions from Mexico and Texas all the way to northern California. The combination of Spanish and Native American cultures created the Southwestern cuisine that we know and love today, including Tex-Mex—recipes that combine foods from Texas and Mexico and often include spicy chilies. Most Southwestern dishes originated with the Aztecs (Native Americans of central Mexico), but were later given Spanish names by Spanish

explorers and conquerors. The Spanish introduced oils and frying to the Aztecs. Today, frying is used in many Southwestern recipes.

The American Southwest has some of the most flavorful and colorful foods of anywhere in the United States. It also has some of the most nutritious food because it uses vitamin-rich ingredients such as beans, corn, and fresh vegetables. Corn—one of the staples of Southwestern cuisine—was one of the first field crops grown by Southwestern Native Americans and became their most important food. In fact, historians believe that 80 percent of the diet of these early peoples came from some form of maize (corn). Soon, other crops such as beans, squash, tomatoes, peppers, and onions were also growing in Southwestern gardens. All of these are still main ingredients in Southwestern cooking.

Southwestern foods can be hot and spicy or sweet and salty. They may be vegetarian or stuffed with plenty of meat and cheese. Just about every Southwestern dish can be adapted to personal tastes. That's what makes Southwestern cooking so much fun. Every time you make something, you can create your own culinary masterpiece.

Did you know that Southwestern cuisine has some of the oldest recipes in America? People in this region were making tacos and tamales long before European settlers came to Jamestown and Plymouth.

Kitchen Safety

For successful cooking, be sure to read the recipe all the way through before you start. Assemble the ingredients and tools you'll need before you begin, and your projects will be much more fun.

Make certain your hair is tied back, your sleeves are rolled up for most cooking but down when frying, and your hands are washed. Wear oven mitts when handling anything hot. Stoves, ovens, and sharp items, such as knives and graters, should be used only under adult supervision.

Some of these recipes call for jalapeños and other hot peppers. Wear kitchen gloves when handling these peppers, and be sure not to touch your face, especially your eyes. The seeds are the hottest parts of these peppers; use them to taste, but moderation is the key.

Avocados are used in hand creams and shampoos as well as in Southwestern cooking. They also make a fun ice cream flavor.

Guacamole

Avocado trees thrive in the warm climate of the Southwest, making avocados plentiful. People eat these creamy fruits sliced on toast and crackers and tossed into salads. They add them instead of cheese to scrambled eggs. They also mash them and mix them with lemon juice and spices to make a dip for tortilla chips called guacamole (gwah-kuh-MOH-lee). Here's an easy guacamole recipe that requires very few ingredients.

Preparation Time: 10 minutes
Serves: 4

Ingredients

2 ripe avocados
3 tablespoons lemon juice
1 tablespoon green onions, chopped
Salt
Pepper
Medium or hot salsa (optional)

1. Cut the avocados in half. Remove the seeds with a spoon.
2. Scoop the avocado meat out of the shells. Throw away the shells, but keep the seeds.
3. In a small bowl, mash the avocado with a fork.
4. Stir in the lemon juice and onions. Add salt and pepper to taste.
5. For spicier guacamole, add ½ cup salsa.

To store any leftovers, lay plastic wrap directly on the dip, then cover the bowl with a lid. Some people believe that sinking an avocado seed halfway into the guacamole helps keep it from turning brown. You can use the seeds you saved in this recipe to test that theory. Store guacamole in the refrigerator for up to two days.

Salsa

Salsa dates back hundreds of years in the Southwest. In Spanish, *salsa* means "sauce." This dip is primarily made of tomatoes, onions, peppers, cilantro, and lime or lemon juice. Depending upon the region and the cook who makes it, salsa can also include ingredients such as beans and corn or fruit (such as mangoes, peaches, or pineapple).

Salsa can be made using vegetables from your garden or from the grocery store's fresh produce department.

Preparation Time: 15 to 20 minutes
Serves: 4

Ingredients

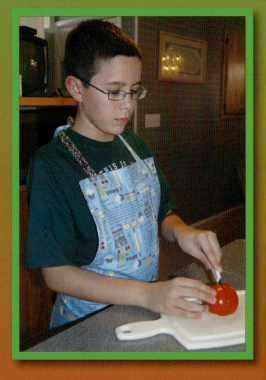

4 tablespoons fresh cilantro
2 ripe tomatoes, diced
1 bell pepper (any color), seeded
   and diced
2–3 jalapeño peppers, seeded
   and diced (see red tip box)
1 small onion, diced
¼ cup lemon juice or limejuice
Salt
Pepper

1. Use a pair of kitchen shears (scissors) to trim cilantro into small pieces.
2. Scoop all chopped ingredients into a medium-sized bowl.
3. Pour in lime or lemon juice. Add salt and pepper to taste. Mix well.

Serve as a side dish with tortilla chips or as a topping for other Southwestern dishes. Store in the refrigerator.

To cut jalapeños, put on a pair of plastic or rubber kitchen gloves, because the juice and seeds of the jalapeño can burn your skin. Remove the stems from the jalapeños. Cut the peppers in half lengthwise and scrape out the seeds. Dice the jalapeños into small pieces. Throw away the extra-spicy seeds, or use them sparingly.

For black bean and corn salsa, add ½ cup black beans and ½ cup fresh or frozen corn (thawed).

For fruit salsa, add ½ cup diced mangoes or ½ cup diced peaches.

For milder salsa, decrease the number of jalapeño peppers.

For spicier salsa, increase the number of jalapeño peppers or add a few of the seeds.

Black Beans

Beans and rice are staples in Southwestern cooking. Some people prefer mashed pinto beans (refried beans), while others like whole black beans. Not only are beans served over rice, they are also served in taco salads, inside burritos, and as a dip for tortilla chips.

Beans are high in nutritional value. They have a lot of protein, fiber, and vitamins. In many recipes, they are prepared with a little oil and fat, but these are not required to make this tasty dish.

Preparation Time: 5 minutes
Cooking Time: Approximately 1 hour
Serves: 4 to 6

Ingredients

1 can black beans, with liquid
1 clove garlic, chopped
2 tablespoons parsley flakes
3 tablespoons white vinegar
1 teaspoon cumin
½ cup onion, diced
¼ cup water
Salt and pepper to taste

1. Combine all the ingredients in a small pot.
2. Cook on low heat for about 1 hour. Stir occasionally so that the beans don't stick to the bottom.
3. When the juices thicken, the beans are done.

For spicy beans, add 1 or 2 jalapeño peppers, seeded and chopped.

11

Refried Beans

Refried beans are a traditional dish in both Mexican and Tex-Mex meals. Essentially, the beans are boiled, and then they are mashed and cooked with fat or oil. Many people buy canned refried beans from the store, but this dish tastes even better when you prepare it at home. Many times, refried beans are made with lard (animal fat). This vegetarian recipe is made with a healthier fat: olive oil.

Preparation Time: 15 to 20 minutes
Cooking Time: 4 hours
Serves: 8 to 10

Ingredients

2½ cups dried pinto beans
3 quarts water
½ cup chopped onion
¼ cup water
2 tablespoon olive oil
Salt and pepper to taste
Cheddar cheese (optional)

1. Rinse the beans in water. Remove any small stones or bad beans.
2. Pour beans into a medium-sized pot and cover completely with water.
3. Cook over medium heat for 3 hours or until beans are tender.
4. Drain off the water using a strainer.
5. Return the beans to the pot. Mash them with a potato masher.
6. Place the beans back on the stovetop and add the onions, water, and oil. Cook until the mixture starts to thicken.
7. Add salt and pepper to taste. If desired, top with cheddar cheese.

For spicy beans, add 1 to 2 jalapeño peppers, seeded and chopped, when you add the onions.

13

Spanish Rice

Rice, called *arroz* in Spanish, accompanies most traditional Southwestern dishes. It can be plain white and mixed with beans, or topped with grated cheese and sour cream. It can also be prepared with tomato sauce and seasonings for a spicy dish called Spanish rice or Mexican rice. This dish is usually served as a side dish with enchiladas, tacos, or tamales. It can also be served in a taco salad or rolled into a stuffed burrito.

Preparation Time: 5 to 10 minutes
Cooking Time: 30 minutes
Serves: 8 to 10

Ingredients

5 beef bouillon cubes
1 tablespoon chili powder
1½ teaspoons ground cumin
½ teaspoon garlic powder
½ teaspoon salt
2 tablespoons butter
5 cups water
6–8 ounces tomato sauce or
    spicy tomato sauce (such as El Pato brand)
3 cups rice, uncooked

1. Place all ingredients except the rice into a medium-sized pot. Bring to a boil over medium heat.
2. When bouillon cubes have dissolved, turn the heat to simmer and add rice.
3. Cover the pot and cook for 20 minutes. Do not open the lid at all during this time.
4. When the rice is done, fluff it with a fork before serving.

Creamy Carrot Soup

I first had carrot soup at an authentic Mexican restaurant in Los Angeles, California, years ago. Now my family includes it as a side dish for our Southwestern-themed suppers. It also works well as a main dish, served with buttered bread. Carrot soup is actually a traditional dish of Puebla, a colonial city in central Mexico.

Preparation Time: 15 minutes
Cooking Time: About 1 hour
Serves: 6 to 8

Ingredients

¼ cup butter or margarine
¼–½ cup chopped onion
2 cups thinly sliced carrots
½ teaspoon salt
3 cups hot chicken broth
¼ cup rice
2 cups half-and-half
Chives, chopped (optional)

1. Melt butter in a large skillet. Add onion and cook until lightly browned.
2. Add carrots and salt. Turn skillet to low heat and cover with a lid. Cook for 20 minutes, stirring occasionally.
3. Scoop cooked carrot mixture into a medium-sized soup pot. Add chicken broth and rice. Cover the pot and cook on very low heat for about 20 minutes, or until rice is done.
4. Scoop soup, a portion at a time, into an electric blender. Blend until smooth. Return the blended soup to the pot.
5. Add half-and-half and cook on low heat for about 10 more minutes. Stir occasionally so that soup doesn't burn.
6. Sprinkle each serving with chopped chives, if desired.

Tortilla Soup

Tortillas—"little cakes" of flour or cornmeal—have been made in the Americas for thousands of years. They are eaten plain, topped with beans and cheese and rolled into burritos, baked into taco bowls, or fried into chips. Where other cultures have used bread, the Native Americans have used tortillas. In the year 1540, Spanish conquistador Francisco Vásquez de Coronado led an expedition to the American Southwest. He reported to the Spanish governor in Mexico that the Pueblos who lived there "made the best tortillas that I have ever seen anywhere, and this is what everybody ordinarily eats."

For this recipe, corn tortillas are used to thicken a pot of chicken soup. If you want, crunchy fried tortilla chips can be added to the soup when you serve it.

Preparation Time: 5 minutes
Cooking Time: 30 to 40 minutes
Serves: 4 to 6

Ingredients

1½ pounds boneless skinless chicken breasts, diced
1 cup salsa
1 can black beans, drained
1 can corn, drained
1 can green chilis
1 teaspoon garlic salt
⅛ teaspoon pepper
½ teaspoon cumin
2 cups chicken broth
8 corn tortillas, cut into long strips

1. Brown the chicken in a soup pot.
2. Stir in the rest of the ingredients except the tortillas. Cook on low for 20 to 30 minutes, or until the chicken is tender.

Top soup with more tortilla strips, grated cheddar cheese, and sour cream.

3. Add tortilla strips to the soup. Stir until they dissolve. This thickens the soup.

Catalina Salad

This salad—a slightly spicy combination of corn chips and beans—is popular at summertime barbecues and potlucks. It can be served alone for a light lunch or as a side dish for dinner. A terrific soup-and-salad combo: Catalina Salad and Creamy Carrot Soup.

Preparation Time: 10 to 15 minutes
Serves: 8

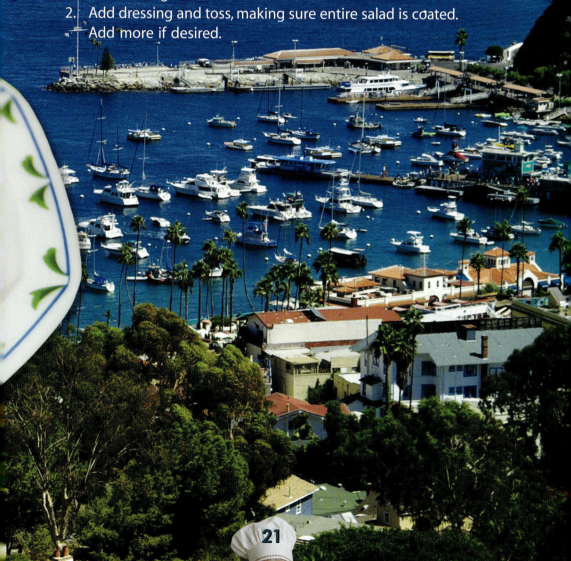

Ingredients

1 can kidney beans, drained
1 cup grated cheddar cheese
½ cup celery
½ cup chopped green pepper
½ cup chopped green onions
1 cup corn chips (such as Fritos brand)
1 small can diced black olives
1 cup Catalina dressing (also called California-style French)

1. In a mixing bowl, stir all ingredients together except for the dressing.
2. Add dressing and toss, making sure entire salad is coated. Add more if desired.

Catalina dressing is like French dressing, only spicier.

Red Pimiento Potatoes

This recipe for Red Pimiento Potatoes serves as a great side for either spicy or mild entrées. The pimiento is a type of red pepper. If you prefer spicier potatoes, swap the pimiento for chopped chili peppers or jalapeños.

Preparation Time: 10 to 15 minutes
Cooking Time: 30 minutes
Serves: 8 to 10

Ingredients

1 32-ounce bag frozen southern-style potatoes
1 10-ounce can cream of mushroom soup
1 10-ounce can cream of celery soup
1 cup milk
1 cup cubed cheddar cheese
2 tablespoons green pepper, chopped
2 tablespoons onion, chopped
1 small jar pimientos
1 cup buttered breadcrumbs

1. Preheat oven to 350°F.
2. Pour all ingredients except for the breadcrumbs into a large mixing bowl. Stir until mixed well.
3. Scoop mixture into a greased 9 x 13-inch casserole dish. Top with buttered breadcrumbs.
4. Bake for 30 minutes or until the top is brown and bubbly.

Chili con Queso

Chili con queso means "chili with cheese." The name is used for a dish that combines beef-and-beans chili with lots of melted cheese, and for a dish that mixes chili peppers with cheese sauce. Also known as just "queso," this dip is a common appetizer at Tex-Mex restaurants. To some people, it is also known as nacho cheese sauce. It started out in Texas cooking, but now it can be found in restaurants and grocery stores across the country.

There are many ways to make queso at home. Here is one of the simplest.

Preparation Time: 10 minutes
Cooking Time: Approximately 1 hour in a slow cooker; about 5 minutes in the microwave
Serves: 8 to 10

Ingredients

2 pounds Velveeta® cheese food, cubed
1 small onion, diced
2 medium tomatoes, diced
¾ cup salsa
2 cans nacho cheese soup
¼ cup milk

1. Place the cheese in a slow cooker or in a microwave-safe dish. Cook on low heat until cheese is melted.
2. Add the rest of the ingredients except for the milk. Heat through, stirring often. Add milk to thin the mixture as needed.
3. Serve hot with tortilla chips. You can also drizzle the queso on scrambled eggs, hamburgers, tacos, or burritos. Refrigerate leftover queso and reheat in the microwave.

For spicier dip, add some jarred jalapeño slices.

Brunch Eggs Olé

In the Southwest, breakfast dishes are often served with a side of salsa. Huevos Rancheros (ranch-style eggs), for example, are scrambled or fried eggs served on hot tortillas and smothered with salsa. Brunch Eggs Olé is a cheesy egg casserole topped with salsa, but it is also good plain or with ketchup if you prefer a milder start to your day. This dish can also be served for lunch or dinner.

Preparation Time: 15 minutes
Cooking Time: 45 to 50 minutes
Serves: 8 to 10

Ingredients

8 eggs
½ cup flour
1 teaspoon baking powder
¾ teaspoon salt
2 cups shredded Monterey Jack cheese
1½ cup (12 ounces) small-curd
    cottage cheese
1 cup shredded sharp cheddar cheese
2 teaspoon hot pepper sauce (optional)
Salsa (optional)

1. Preheat oven to 350°F.
2. Grease a 9-inch-square baking pan.
3. Beat eggs in a large bowl at high speed with an electric mixer for 4 to 5 minutes.
4. Combine flour, baking powder, and salt in a small bowl.
5. Stir flour mixture into eggs until blended.
6. Combine Monterey Jack cheese, cottage cheese, cheddar cheese, and hot pepper sauce (if desired) in a medium bowl. Mix well.
7. Fold the cheeses into the egg mixture until well blended.
8. Pour into prepared pan.
9. Bake 45 to 50 minutes or until golden brown and firm in center.
10. Let stand 10 minutes before cutting into squares. Top each square with salsa, if desired.

Breakfast Burritos

Not only are eggs often topped with salsa in the Southwest, but they are also rolled into a flour tortilla and served as a burrito. These "breakfast" burritos can be served at any time of day.

Preparation Time: 5 to 10 minutes
Cooking Time: 15 minutes
Serves: 1

Ingredients

2 eggs
¼ cup milk
Crumbled bacon,
    ham, cooked sausage,
    tomatoes, or potatoes (optional)
2 tablespoons butter
1 flour tortilla
¼ cup shredded cheddar cheese or cheese of choice
Salsa

1. In a small mixing bowl, beat the eggs and milk together. Stir in any of the optional ingredients you'd like.
2. Melt the butter in a skillet and add the egg mixture. Cook on low heat, stirring gently, until done.
3. Place a tortilla on a plate and warm it in the microwave for 10 to 15 seconds.
4. Scoop the cooked eggs onto the tortilla near an outside edge.
5. Sprinkle cheese on top.
6. Fold one edge of the tortilla over the mixture. Roll the tortilla over the top of the mixture until you reach the other end. Place seam-side down on a plate.
7. Sprinkle cheese and salsa on top of burrito, if desired.

Quesadillas

Quesadillas are cheese-stuffed round tortillas that have been cut into triangles, like a pizza. They can be filled with just cheese—as this recipe calls for—or stuffed with other ingredients such as seasoned chicken, avocados, or tomatoes. Each quesadilla requires two tortillas. Quesadillas can be served as a main dish or as an appetizer.

Preparation Time: 5 minutes
Cooking Time: 3 to 5 minutes
Serves: 1

Ingredients

2 flour tortillas,
   any size
½ cup grated cheese
Toppings: sour cream,
   salsa, guacamole

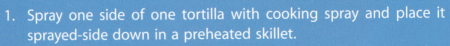

1. Spray one side of one tortilla with cooking spray and place it sprayed-side down in a preheated skillet.
2. Layer the tortilla with grated cheese and top with the other tortilla.
3. Spray this top tortilla with cooking spray.
4. Cook over medium heat for 2 to 4 minutes.
5. Carefully turn it over and cook this side until golden brown.
6. Remove from skillet and place on a cutting board or plate. Cut into wedges.
7. Add your choice of toppings, such as sour cream, salsa, or guacamole.

Tacos

In Mexico, tacos were traditionally just a light meal or snack. They are similar in idea to the sandwich. Instead of placing meat or cheese between two pieces of bread like a sandwich, people place meat inside a tortilla to make a taco.

Tacos can be made in a variety of ways. They are generally filled with seasoned ground beef or shredded chicken; you can also use ground turkey, beans, fish, or tofu. You can use packaged seasonings from the store, or you can make this tastier version with a few ingredients from a standard spice rack. You can make them with soft flour tortillas, soft corn tortillas, or deep-fried hard corn tortillas. Cheese and other toppings may also be added.

Preparation Time: 10 minutes
Cooking Time: 15 to 20 minutes
Serves: 6

Ingredients

Taco Meat
1 pound ground beef,
    ground turkey, or
    shredded cooked chicken
1 onion, chopped
2 cloves garlic, chopped
4-ounce can diced green chilies
1 tablespoon chili powder
1 teaspoon cumin
½ teaspoon rosemary
¼ teaspoon salt

1. In a medium skillet, cook the ground beef or turkey and onion until the meat is brown and the onion is clear. If you are using shredded cooked chicken, sauté just the onion.

2. Drain grease if needed.
3. Add the rest of the ingredients and cook for another 10 to 15 minutes on medium heat. Stir often.

For each taco
1 preformed hard corn taco shell
¼ cup taco meat
Your choice of toppings, such as grated cheese,
    guacamole, sour cream, lettuce,
    black olives, and salsa

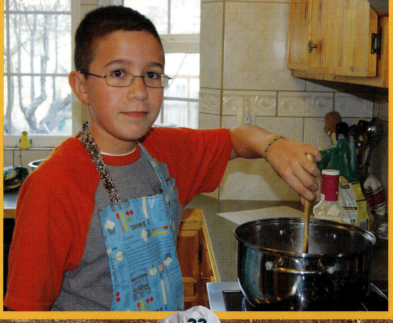

1. Place a taco shell on a plate.
2. Fill it with taco meat.
3. Sprinkle cheese on top of the meat, then add your other favorite toppings.

You can also make a double-layer taco: Spread ¼ cup refried beans on a flour tortilla that is slightly larger than the hard taco shell. Heat in microwave for 20 seconds. Wrap it around the shell of the hard taco.

Taco Salad in Baked Taco Bowls

At Southwestern restaurants, taco salad is usually served in a deep-fried flour tortilla bowl. This recipe shows you how to make a low-fat version of this kind of bowl that is just as crispy as the deep-fried variety.

Preparation Time: 5 minutes
Cooking Time: 10 to 15 minutes
Serves: 4

Ingredients

4 large burrito-size flour tortillas
1 tablespoon butter or margarine, melted
Salad vegetables such as lettuce, diced tomatoes, and avocados or guacamole
Taco meat (see page 32)
Spanish rice (see page 14)
Black beans or refried beans (see pages 10 and 12)
Grated cheddar cheese
Sour cream
Sliced black olives

1. Preheat oven to 400°F.
2. Melt butter in a small bowl in the microwave.
3. Warm tortillas in the microwave for about 30 seconds.
4. Brush melted butter onto both sides of the tortillas.

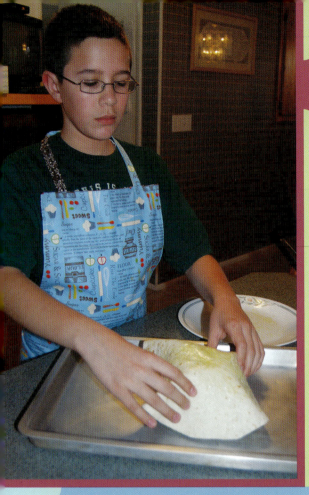

You can also use whole-wheat, spinach, or sundried-tomato tortillas.

5. Turn 4 oven-safe soup bowls upside down on a baking sheet and drape a tortilla shell over each bowl. Press the tortilla down on the bowl so that it forms to the shape of the bowl.
6. Bake for 10 to 15 minutes, until shells are golden brown.
7. Let cool.
8. Remove tortillas from the bowls. They should now be baked into a bowl shape.
9. Fill each tortilla bowl with any of the listed ingredients to make a taco salad.

Cut corn tortillas into 1-inch-wide strips and bake in a single layer with the bowls (do not butter them). Add these crispy strips to the top of your salads.

36

Nachos

Nachos are a popular Southwestern appetizer or snack. They consist of tortilla chips covered in melted cheese and a variety of toppings such as taco meat, beans, sour cream, and guacamole. Nachos don't have to be just an appetizer, though. They also make a hearty lunch or dinner.

Preparation Time: 5 minutes
Cooking Time: 3 to 5 minutes
Serves: 2 or more

Ingredients

Tortilla chips
Shredded cheddar cheese (or Mexican blend cheese)
Hot toppings, such as black beans, refried beans, or taco meat
Cold toppings, such as guacamole, sour cream, jalapeños, onions, tomatoes, lettuce, black olives, or salsa

1. Preheat oven to 350°F.
2. Spread one layer of tortilla chips over a baking sheet. Place random spoonfuls of the beans and meat (if desired) on the chips. Sprinkle everything with the shredded cheese.
3. Cook in the oven for several minutes or until cheese is completely melted.
4. Scoop the chips onto plates or a platter and add any cold toppings you desire.

Burritos

Historians believe that the burrito was invented in northern Mexico in the 1840s. It was meant to be a way for ranchers and miners to take a meal to work. The original burrito was just a chunk of spicy meat wrapped inside a flour tortilla. These handy meals came to be called "little burros" (burros are a type of pack animal) because they could carry just about anything.

Burritos are always made with flour tortillas, never corn tortillas. They most often hold beans (either refried or black), but they can also be filled with shredded chicken, pork, and beef; cheese; and even potatoes. They can be served plain or topped with enchilada sauce and cheese and baked. This recipe shows you how to make a bean, beef, and cheese burrito.

Preparation Time: 5 minutes
Cooking Time: 1 minute
Serves: 1

Ingredients

1 burrito-sized flour tortilla
½ cup refried beans, heated
¼ cup taco meat, heated
¼ cup grated cheddar cheese

1. Place the flour tortilla on a plate and heat it in the microwave for 10 to 15 seconds.
2. Scoop beans and meat along one side of the tortilla. Sprinkle these with cheese.
3. Fold in the ends of the tortilla, then roll the tortilla over the top of the mixture until you reach the other side. Place seam-side down on a plate.
4. Sprinkle with cheese and enchilada sauce (if desired; see page 42) and cook in the microwave for another 10 to 15 seconds, until the cheese is melted.

Chicken Enchiladas

Enchilada means "filled with chili," and the Aztecs may have invented the dish. Enchiladas are corn or flour tortillas that have been dipped in chili sauce, then rolled around a filling of cheese, chicken, beef, or pork. They are usually smothered with more green or red chili sauce and baked in a casserole dish. Another traditional way to make them involves layering the tortillas, cheese, and sauce, then topping the whole pile with onions, lettuce, and a fried egg. Enchiladas can be mild, spicy, or sweet. This particular recipe is for a sweet version of chicken enchiladas covered with a red sauce made with brown sugar and salsa. While you can cook the chicken in less time in a regular soup pot, it will turn out more tender and will be easier to shred if you use a slow cooker.

Preparation Time: 3 hours + 15 minutes
Cooking Time: 30 minutes
Serves: 5 to 6 (makes 10 to 12 enchiladas)

Ingredients

2 cups salsa
½ cup brown sugar
2–3 pounds chicken breast
10–12 flour tortillas
Grated cheddar cheese
Sour cream and salsa (optional)

1. In a medium-size bowl, mix salsa and brown sugar together.
2. Spray a slow cooker with cooking oil. Place the chicken in the slow cooker and pour the salsa mixture on top.
3. Cook on low until the chicken is tender and falling off the bone, usually about 3 hours.
4. Remove chicken and let it cool slightly in the refrigerator. Keep the juices in the slow cooker. You will use them later.

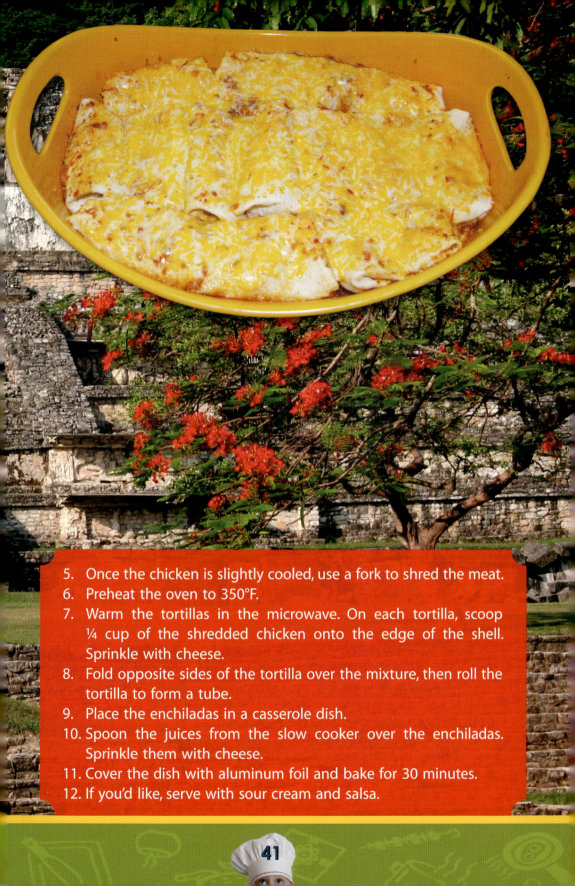

5. Once the chicken is slightly cooled, use a fork to shred the meat.
6. Preheat the oven to 350°F.
7. Warm the tortillas in the microwave. On each tortilla, scoop ¼ cup of the shredded chicken onto the edge of the shell. Sprinkle with cheese.
8. Fold opposite sides of the tortilla over the mixture, then roll the tortilla to form a tube.
9. Place the enchiladas in a casserole dish.
10. Spoon the juices from the slow cooker over the enchiladas. Sprinkle them with cheese.
11. Cover the dish with aluminum foil and bake for 30 minutes.
12. If you'd like, serve with sour cream and salsa.

Enchilada Sauce

Ingredients

¼ cup vegetable oil
2 tablespoons flour
¼ cup chili powder
1 8-ounce can tomato sauce
1½ cups water
¼ teaspoon ground cumin
¼ teaspoon garlic powder
¼ teaspoon onion salt
Salt to taste

Preparation Time: 5 minutes
Cooking Time: About 12 minutes
Serves: 4 to 6

1. In a skillet, mix oil, flour, and chili powder. Stir constantly over medium-high heat so as not to burn the flour. Cook until lightly browned, about 2 minutes.
2. Turn the heat down to medium-low. Slowly stir in the remaining ingredients, except the salt.
3. Mix until smooth and cook for about 10 minutes or until the sauce thickens.
4. Add salt to taste.

1. Enchiladas with side of beans
2. Tamale pie with side of beans
3. Chimichanga (deep-fried burrito) with side of beans
4. Chicken quesadillas with side of beans
5. Chicken taco salad

Fajitas

Fajitas are usually made with either grilled chicken or steak. When you order them at a Mexican restaurant, the meat will usually come out on a sizzling cast-iron skillet with warmed tortillas on the side so that you can assemble your own meal tableside. You can put these homemade fajitas together before you serve them, or you can place everything on the table separately and let people assemble their own.

Preparation Time: 45 minutes + 1 hour to marinate
Cooking Time: 20 to 25 minutes
Serves: 4

Ingredients

1 pound boneless skinless
    chicken breasts, cut into
    ¼-inch strips; OR
    1 pound skirt steak
Fajita marinade (below)
1 tablespoon canola oil
1 cup onion, slivered
1 cup bell pepper, slivered
8 flour tortillas (6-inch size)
Toppings such as shredded Monterey Jack
    cheese or Mexican blend, shredded lettuce,
    chopped tomatoes, salsa, guacamole, and sour cream

Marinade
Juice of 1 lime
2 tablespoons olive oil
2 cloves garlic, peeled and minced
½ teaspoon ground cumin
½ fresh jalapeño pepper, seeded and chopped (see page 9)
¼ cup chopped fresh cilantro, including stems

1. In a large resealable bag, place the meat and marinade ingredients. Seal the bag. Gently shake the bag to coat the meat. Refrigerate for one hour or longer.
2. Add the oil to a large skillet. Add the meat and cook. (Throw away the bag and the marinade.) The chicken is done when it is no longer pink. You can cook the steak rarer if you'd like, as long as the internal temperature is at least 165°F.
3. Move the meat to a plate and cover loosely with foil. Let it rest for 10 minutes.
4. Meanwhile, sauté the onion and bell pepper for 3 minutes or until tender.
5. If you are making steak fajitas, ask an adult to cut the steak into very thin strips. Cutting the steak at an angle, across the grain, will make the meat more tender.
6. Warm the tortillas in the microwave.
7. Spoon some of the meat and some of the onion mixture into the center of each tortilla and fold over. Continue until all are filled.
8. Add the toppings of your choice.

Quick Tamale Pie

In Southwest cooking, corn takes on many forms besides tortillas. For example, traditional tamales contain a corn-based dough called masa. They are wrapped in cornhusks and roasted. In this recipe, corn kernels are used in the casserole, and corn muffins are crumbled on top, with whole corn muffins served on the side.

Preparation Time: 45 to 60 minutes
Cooking Time: 20 minutes
Serves: 8 to 10

Ingredients

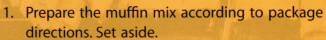

2 boxes corn muffin mix
   (check box for any other ingredients
   you'll need to prepare the muffins)
1½ pounds ground beef or turkey
¾ cup sliced green onions
4-ounce can green chilies, drained
1 can tomato soup
¾ cup salsa
16-ounce can corn, drained
2¼-ounce can black olives, drained
1 tablespoon Worcestershire sauce
1 teaspoon chili powder
¼ teaspoon garlic powder
1 cup grated cheddar cheese

1. Prepare the muffin mix according to package directions. Set aside.
2. Preheat oven to 350°F.
3. In a skillet, brown the ground beef or turkey, green onions, and chilies.
4. When beef is brown, add tomato soup, salsa, corn, olives, Worcestershire sauce, chili powder, and garlic powder.

5. Pour into a greased 2-quart casserole dish.
6. On top of the casserole, sprinkle cheese.
7. Crumble 4 of the muffins on top of the cheese.
8. Place the casserole in the oven. Bake for 10 minutes or until cheese is melted.
9. Scoop onto plates and top with sour cream and salsa (if desired). Serve with the rest of the corn muffins.

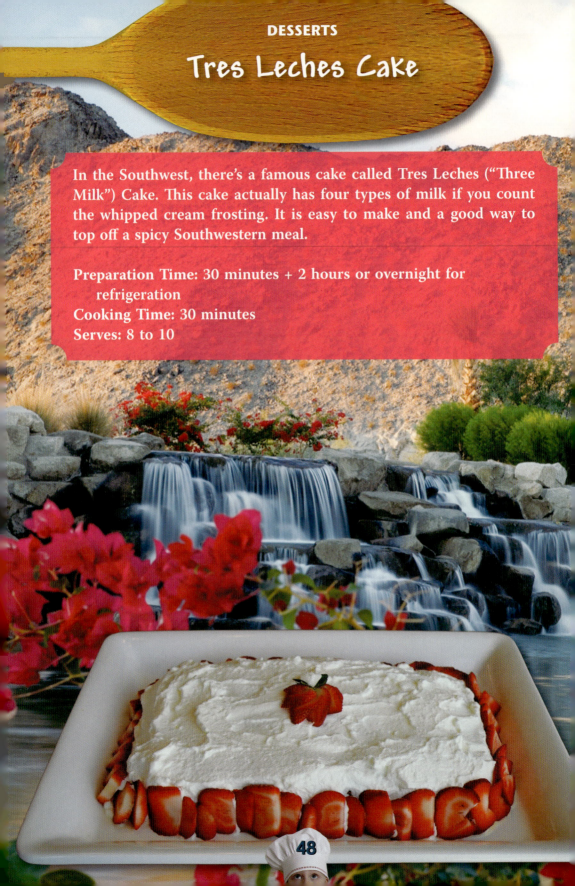

Tres Leches Cake

In the Southwest, there's a famous cake called Tres Leches ("Three Milk") Cake. This cake actually has four types of milk if you count the whipped cream frosting. It is easy to make and a good way to top off a spicy Southwestern meal.

Preparation Time: 30 minutes + 2 hours or overnight for refrigeration
Cooking Time: 30 minutes
Serves: 8 to 10

Cake
½ cup unsalted butter
1 cup sugar
5 eggs
½ teaspoon vanilla extract
1½ cups all-purpose flour
1 teaspoon baking powder

Tres Leches
2 cups whole milk
1 14-ounce can sweetened
   condensed milk
1 12-ounce can evaporated
   milk

Whipped Cream Frosting
1½ cups heavy whipping cream
1 cup white sugar
1 teaspoon vanilla extract

1. Preheat oven to 350°F.
2. Grease and flour a 9 x 13-inch baking pan.
3. Cream butter and 1 cup sugar together until fluffy.
4. Add eggs and ½ teaspoon vanilla; beat well.
5. Add flour and baking powder; mix well.
6. Pour into pan and bake for 30 minutes.
7. When cake is slightly cooled, pierce it several times with a fork.
8. In a mixing bowl, combine the *tres leches*. Slowly pour this mixture over the cooled cake.
9. Place the cake in the refrigerator for at least 2 hours or overnight.
10. Combine the ingredients for the whipped cream frosting. Whip until thick.
11. Spread over the cake.
12. Serve. Store leftovers in the refrigerator.

Mexican Wedding Cookies

In many traditional cultures, foods like cakes and cookies that require expensive ingredients (such as sugar and butter) were often made only on special occasions. The Mexican Wedding Cookie is one of those types of recipes. It is made almost entirely of butter and sugar and is traditionally served at weddings or at Christmastime. This cookie isn't only made in the Mexican culture, however. Historians think people in the Middle East were the first to make the cookie hundreds of years ago. Then, the dessert eventually spread throughout Europe and America. This cookie is also called Russian Tea Cakes. Regardless of where they came from, Mexican Wedding Cookies are definitely a favorite treat in the modern American Southwest.

Preparation Time: 20 minutes
Cooking Time: 10 to 12 minutes
Makes: 4 dozen cookies

Ingredients

- 1 cup butter or margarine, softened
- ½ cup confectioners' sugar
- 1 teaspoon vanilla
- ¼ teaspoon salt
- 2¼ cups flour
- ¾ cup finely chopped walnuts or pecans
- Confectioners' sugar for rolling after the cookies have baked

1. Heat oven to 400°F.
2. In a large bowl, mix the butter, confectioners' sugar, and vanilla until smooth.
3. Stir in the salt and flour, and then mix in the nuts.
4. Scoop a teaspoon of dough into your clean hands. Shape the dough into a ball by rolling it between your palms. Each ball should be about 1 inch across.
5. Place the balls about 1 inch apart on an ungreased cookie sheet. Do not flatten them.
6. Bake cookies for 10 to 12 minutes. They should still be white, not brown, when you take them out of the oven.
7. With a spatula, remove the cookies from the cookie sheet. Cool them slightly on a wire rack.
8. While the cookies are still warm, roll them on a plate of confectioners' sugar.
9. Let them cool completely on the wire rack.
10. Roll them in confectioners' sugar again and serve.

Flan

The ancient Romans began making flan, a type of custard, when they started keeping chickens and needed to find a way to use the extra eggs. They made savory flan with fish and herbs; or they made sweet flan with almonds and honey or with fruit. The Spanish added a caramelized topping to the custard. They brought his sweet dish to the New World, and it has remained popular throughout Mexico and the American Southwest.

Preparation Time: 20 minutes
Cooking Time: 1 hour + 1 hour
to cool
Serves: 6

Ingredients

1 cup + ½ cup sugar
6 large eggs
1 14-ounce can sweetened
condensed milk
2 13-ounce cans evaporated
milk
1 teaspoon vanilla

1. Preheat oven to 325°F.
2. Pour 1 cup of the sugar into a saucepan over medium heat. Stir the sugar constantly until it melts, browns, and turns to caramel.
3. Quickly scoop 2 to 3 tablespoons of the caramel into each of six ramekins (small round Pyrex or ceramic dishes that can be baked in the oven). Tilt each ramekin so that the caramel covers the bottom of it. If the caramel becomes hard in the pan, you'll have to reheat it.
4. In a mixing bowl, add the eggs, both kinds of milk, the remaining sugar, and vanilla. Whisk until smooth.

5. Pour this mixture evenly into the ramekins.
6. Place the ramekins in the baking dish. Fill the baking dish with about 1 to 2 inches of hot water. Ask an adult to carefully put the dish in the oven.
7. Bake for 45 minutes. To check for doneness, insert the tip of a knife in the center of the flan. If the knife comes out clean, the flan is done.
8. Ask an adult to remove the pan from the oven. Let it cool for one hour.
9. To serve, tip each ramekin onto a small plate and let the golden caramel sauce flow over the cream-colored custard. Do not scrape the ramekin.

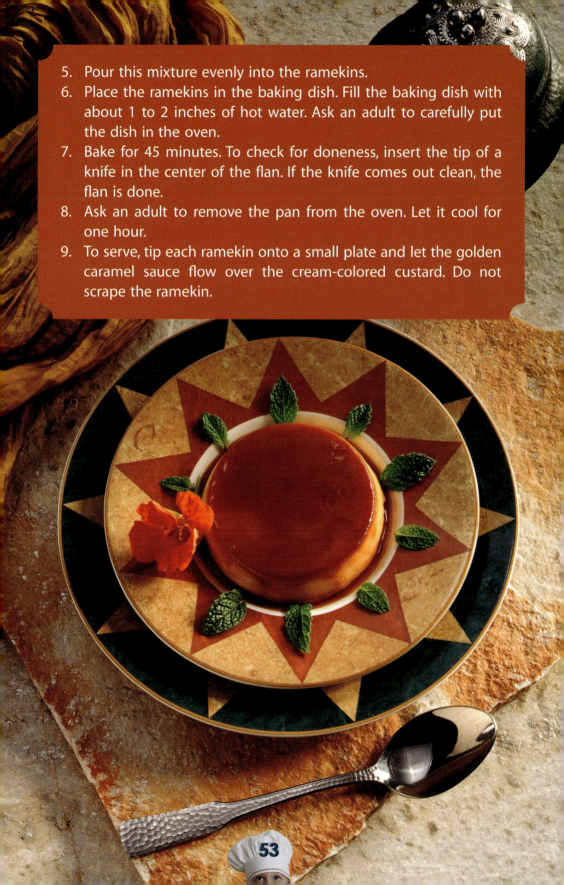

New Year's Eve Flautas

When I was a child, New Year's Eve was a time to spend with family and eat a variety of Southwestern dishes. Flautas were a good choice because you could make a lot of them in advance. Similar to taquitos, flautas are usually made with flour tortillas (taquitos are usually made with corn tortillas). People warmed the flautas in the microwave as they wanted them throughout the evening. This recipe doesn't have to be made just for New Year's Eve, though. It can be enjoyed any time of the year.

Preparation Time: 20 to 30 minutes
Cooking Time: 25 minutes
Serves: 10

Ingredients

1½ pounds ground beef or turkey
1 cup (4 ounces) shredded cheddar cheese
1 can (4 ounces) chopped green chilies, drained
½ teaspoon ground cumin
10 flour tortillas (6 inches across)
⅓ cup butter, melted, divided
Shredded lettuce, guacamole, salsa, sour cream

1. Preheat the oven to 500°F.
2. In a large skillet, cook meat over medium heat until no longer pink; drain.
3. Stir in the cheese, chilies, and cumin; set aside.
4. Warm the tortillas in the microwave for 30 to 60 seconds.
5. Brush both sides of the tortillas with some of the butter.
6. Scoop about ⅓ cup meat mixture down the center of each tortilla. Roll up tightly to form a long tube. Place seam-side down in a greased 13 x 9-inch baking pan.
7. Bake, uncovered, for 5 to 7 minutes or until golden brown.
8. Place on a plate and serve with toppings of your choice.

New Mexican Holiday Hot Chocolate

Chocolate is native to the Americas. The Europeans never had chocolate until the Aztecs introduced it to the Spaniards in the 1500s, and it quickly became popular in Europe as well.

Hot chocolate or hot cocoa is now a traditional wintertime drink in many parts of the world. This particular recipe—with honey, cinnamon, and nutmeg—is a favorite in New Mexico. It tastes great during the winter holidays alongside buttery Mexican Wedding Cookies.

Preparation Time: 10 to 15 minutes
Cooking Time: 5 to 10 minutes
Serves: 8

Ingredients

⅓ cup water
⅓ cup honey
5 tablespoons cocoa powder
½ teaspoon ground cinnamon
⅛ teaspoon nutmeg
¼ teaspoon salt
4 cups milk
1 teaspoon vanilla extract
Cinnamon, shaved chocolate, or marshmallows (optional)

1. In a large saucepan, combine the first six ingredients. Bring them to a boil over medium heat, stirring constantly.
2. Turn stovetop to low and slowly add the milk and vanilla.
3. Stir constantly while milk is heating until tiny bubbles form around the edge. Do not let the milk boil.
4. Pour into mugs and top with cinnamon, shaved chocolate, or marshmallows, if desired.

Calabaza en Tacha (Candied Pumpkin)

This dish is popular to serve on the Day of the Dead celebration. The Day of the Dead is a family event that takes place on November 1 and 2. It's a time to remember ancestors who have already passed away and who, according to tradition, visit the earth once a year. During this celebration, family members will visit cemeteries and clean and decorate their ancestors' graves. When they return home, they will dine together on traditional foods. *Calabaza en Tacha*, or candied pumpkin, is one of those dishes.

Preparation Time: 20 minutes
Cooking Time: 1 to 2 hours
Serves: 6

Ingredients

- 1 pumpkin, about 4 to 5 pounds
- 8 cinnamon sticks
- 1 orange, juiced
- 4 cups water
- 5 cups brown sugar
- Cold milk or vanilla ice cream

1. Under adult supervision, carefully cut the pumpkin into 3-inch squares.
2. Remove the seeds and strings from the center of each piece.
3. Cut diamond designs into the pulp. This will allow the pumpkin to absorb the juices in which it will cook.

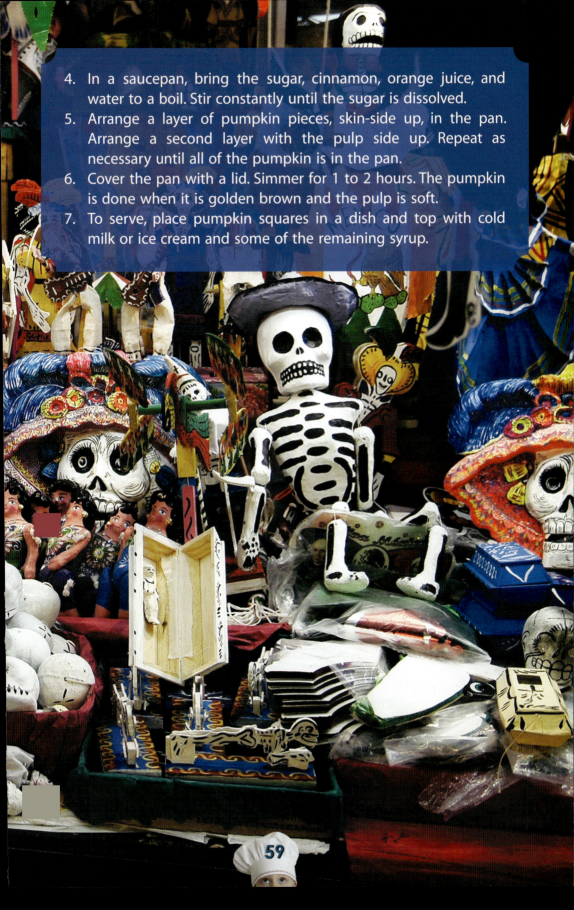

4. In a saucepan, bring the sugar, cinnamon, orange juice, and water to a boil. Stir constantly until the sugar is dissolved.
5. Arrange a layer of pumpkin pieces, skin-side up, in the pan. Arrange a second layer with the pulp side up. Repeat as necessary until all of the pumpkin is in the pan.
6. Cover the pan with a lid. Simmer for 1 to 2 hours. The pumpkin is done when it is golden brown and the pulp is soft.
7. To serve, place pumpkin squares in a dish and top with cold milk or ice cream and some of the remaining syrup.

Further Reading

Books

Betty Crocker's Kids Cook! Minneapolis, MN: General Mills, 2007.

Graimes, Nicola. *Kids' Fun and Healthy Cookbook.* New York: Dorling Kindersley Publishing, 2007.

Hutchins, Vickie, and Jo Ann Martin. *Kids in the Kitchen: Recipes for Fun.* Columbus, Ohio: Gooseberry Patch, 2006.

Karmel, Annabel. *You Can Cook.* New York: Dorling Kindersley Publishing, 2010.

Wilkes, Angela. *The Children's Quick and Easy Cookbook.* New York: DK Children, 2006.

On the Internet

Betty Crocker—Southwest Recipes
    http://www.bettycrocker.com/recipes/global-cuisine/southwest-recipes

Grandma's Cookbook
    http://www.texascooking.com/cookbook.htm

Mexican Food Recipes
    http://www.mexicanfoodrecipes.org/

Southwestern U.S. Recipes
    http://www.food.com/recipes/southwestern-united-states

Superfast Southwestern Recipes
    http://www.cookinglight.com/food/quick-healthy/southwestern-recipes-quick-easy-20-minutes-00400000043359/

Taste of Home—Mexican Recipes
    http://www.tasteofhome.com/Recipes/Cuisine/Mexican-Recipes

Texas Beef Council—Tex-Mex and Southwest Recipes
    http://www.txbeef.org/recipe_book/tex_mex_and_southwest

Further Reading

Works Consulted

Cook, Allison. "Why Chili Con Queso Matters." *Houston Chronicle,* December 27, 2009. http://www.chron.com/disp/story.mpl/life/main/6786526.html

Cusumano, Camille. "Southwestern Cooking." *Via Magazine,* May/June 2001. http://www.viamagazine.com/food-wine/savoring-west-chile-chile-bang-bang

Duggan, Tara. "The Silver Torpedo: The Weighty, One-of-a-Kind Mission Burrito Has Reached Cult Status Among Its Wide Variety of Fans." *SF Gate,* April 29, 2001. http://www.sfgate.com/cgi-bin/article.cgi?f=/c/a/2001/04/29/CM162769.DTL

Ferland, Mallory. "History of Wedding Cakes in Mexico." *USA Today Travel,* n.d. http://traveltips.usatoday.com/history-wedding-cakes-mexico-20313.html

Freeman, Nancy. "Ethnic Cuisine: United States." http://www.sallybernstein.com/food/cuisines/us/

Polaski, Helen. "Mexican Hot Chocolate." http://www.life123.com/food/cocktails-beverages/hot-chocolate/mexican-hot-chocolate.shtml

Smith, Andrew F. "Tacos, Enchiladas, and Refried Beans: The Invention of Mexican-American Cookery." Presented at the Symposium at Oregon State University, 1999. http://web.archive.org/web/20070718154326/http://food.oregonstate.edu/ref/culture/mexico_smith.html

Walker, Judy. "Day of the Dead Food: Festival for Departed Souls Begins with Food." *Arizona Republic,* n.d. http://www.azcentral.com/ent/dead/articles/dead-food.html

Glossary

burrito (bur-EE-toh)—A flour tortilla stuffed with seasoned meat, cheese, and beans.

enchilada (en-chih-LAH-dah)—"Filled with chili": a corn or flour tortilla dipped in chili sauce, then rolled around a filling and baked.

fajita (fah-HEE-tah)—A dish of marinated grilled meat served as strips, with vegetables, inside a flour tortilla.

flauta (FLAOW-tuh)—A rolled-up tortilla stuffed with some type of filling, then baked or deep-fried.

guacamole (gwah-kuh-MOH-lee)—Mashed avocados, spiced and sometimes mixed with tomatoes, served as a dip with tortilla chips or as a topping for Mexican food.

marinate (MAH-rih-nayt)—To soak raw meat in a sauce in order to season it before cooking.

nacho (NAHT-choh)—One in a serving of tortilla chips covered with meat, beans, melted cheese, and other toppings.

quesadilla (kay-suh-DEE-yah)—A grilled cheese sandwich on flour tortillas instead of bread, sometimes with other fillings as well.

queso (KAY-soh)—Cheese.

salsa (SAHL-suh)—A dip made with chopped tomatoes, onions, peppers, and spices such as cilantro. It is served with chips, on top of entrées, or as a side dish.

sauté (saw-TAY)—To fry gently in a light layer of butter or oil in a shallow pan until tender.

taco (TAH-koh)—A traditional Mexican dish made of a corn or wheat tortillas folded or rolled around a filling.

tamale (tah-MAH-lee)—A traditional Latin American dish that is made out of shredded meat stuffed into a corn-based dough called masa and then steamed or boiled in a leaf wrapper.

Tex-Mex (TEKS-MEKS)—A type of cuisine that blends foods from Texas and Mexico and often uses spicy chilies.

tortilla (tor-TEE-yah)—Flat bread made out of corn or flour; the word means "little torta" or "little cake" in Spanish.

Index

About the
AUTHOR

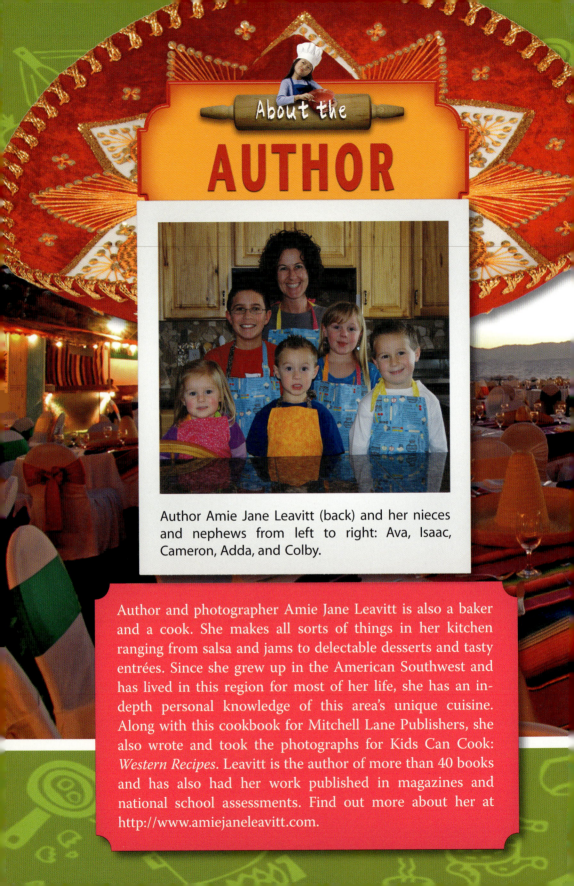

Author Amie Jane Leavitt (back) and her nieces and nephews from left to right: Ava, Isaac, Cameron, Adda, and Colby.

Author and photographer Amie Jane Leavitt is also a baker and a cook. She makes all sorts of things in her kitchen ranging from salsa and jams to delectable desserts and tasty entrées. Since she grew up in the American Southwest and has lived in this region for most of her life, she has an in-depth personal knowledge of this area's unique cuisine. Along with this cookbook for Mitchell Lane Publishers, she also wrote and took the photographs for Kids Can Cook: *Western Recipes*. Leavitt is the author of more than 40 books and has also had her work published in magazines and national school assessments. Find out more about her at http://www.amiejaneleavitt.com.